COME ON, MOM!

75 things for mothers and daughters to do together

written by Cynthia MacGregor

Lobster Press ™

Come on Mom! 75 Things for Mothers and Daughters to Do Together
Text © 2008 Cynthia MacGregor

Published by Lobster Press™
1620 Sherbrooke Street West, Suites C & D
Montréal, Québec   H3H 1C9
Tel. (514) 904-1100 • Fax (514) 904-1101 • www.lobsterpress.com

Publisher: Alison Fripp
Editors: Alison Fripp & Meghan Nolan
Editiorial Assistants: Lindsay Cornish, Nisa Raizen-Miller & Shiran Teitelbaum
Graphic Design & Production: Tammy Desnoyers

Special thanks to Samantha Star of Scrapbook Star, for assistance with the "Scrapbook Nook" section.

Library and Archives Canada Cataloguing in Publication

MacGregor, Cynthia
    Come on, Mom! : 75 things for mothers and daughters to do together / Cynthia MacGregor.

ISBN 978-1-897073-76-6

    1. Family recreation--Juvenile literature. 2. Mothers and daughters--Juvenile literature. I. Title.

GV182.8.M28 2008   j790.1'91   C2007-904818-8

Printed and bound in the United States.

INTRODUCTION

When I was a little girl, I loved doing things with my mom. "Doing things" might mean playing a game of charades or "Go Fish," going out together for ice cream sodas, or even doing the dishes together. Not that I enjoyed drying dishes — my particular chore — but I had the option of drying them while Mom was doing the dish-washing or afterward, and I almost always opted for working alongside her. It gave us some quality Mommy-and-me time, which we sometimes spent just talking as we worked on the dishes but most often spent singing.

I wandered off-key more often than not, and if my mom at least managed to stay on key, that's not to say she had a particularly good voice. But we both *enjoyed* singing, and what's more, we enjoyed singing *together*.

As kids grow older, they may want less one-on-one time with their parents. Mom takes a backseat to friends, homework, and computer games. And of course, few moms today have endless hours at their disposal to play with their kids. Which is why you want to make the time you do spend with them really count.

But, just as my mom and I made doing the dishes

together fun, by singing (or sometimes just talking), or by playing a game such as Geography (see page 22) that required no materials and could be played as we worked in the kitchen, you don't have to spend a lot of money on expensive games or other equipment to have fun.

This book is about mother-daughter fun. I don't mean to slight sons, who are certainly important too, nor am I downplaying the importance of dads to their daughters. But that's not what this book is about. It's about fun that moms and their daughters can have together, whether it's playing a game, or taking an observational walk or drive.

Games for girls don't have to be frilly and fancy, and therefore many of the activities in this book aren't specific to girls. Just as the activities in *Come on, Dad* (Lobster Press), by Ed Avis, aren't all specific to fathers and sons and can be, in many cases, enjoyed by mothers and/or daughters. All of the activities in this book are suitable for mothers and daughters, even if some of them can also be enjoyed by fathers and/or sons.

So make every day "Mother's Day" — or better yet, "Mother/Daughter Day" — by spending a little time with your daughter doing a fun activity. Tell "Progressive Stories" (see page 24) while you set the table together.

Or make it a bedtime activity (see "When I Was a Little Girl," page 113). Or organize a treasure hunt (page 61), just for the fun of it.

Not every activity will suit every mother or every daughter, if only because your daughter may be too young or too old for some of them. But many of them should suit most mothers and daughters. So enjoy them ... and make some memories.

A Note from the Publisher:

As always, please be careful when you and your children participate in the activities listed in this book. The publisher and the author encourage parents to exercise caution and good judgment when engaging in any activity with their children, and neither Lobster Press™ nor the author can be held responsible for any accidents that may occur, or for sickness attributable to allergies or sensitivities.

Table Of Contents

DEAR FUTURE ME

Here's a good activity for a rainy afternoon, or at bedtime. Have your daughter imagine that she's a grown-up, or a teenager. If she's old enough to write, have her write the letter herself, with prompts from you as to what it might contain. What does she want to tell her older self about her life now, her thoughts, her interests, her feelings, her enjoyments, what's important to her, what hurts her, what makes her happy, what intrigues her?

Materials Needed

Pen (or pencil, or computer) and paper

If she's not yet of writing age, have her dictate the letter to you, and you write it down. You can store the letter for safe-keeping to be opened ten or fifteen or twenty years from now, or you can leave it with your daughter, so she can revisit it from time to time.

RADIO REPORTER

*Y*our daughter may or may not have a future as a journalist, but she'll have fun pretending to interview you now. All she needs is a little hand-held tape recorder or other recording device, loaded with a blank tape, and an available interviewee ... you.

There are several variations possible in the way you play this:

⊙ She can pre-script the questions she is going to ask you, or she can "wing it."

⊙ You can pretend to be someone other than yourself, and be interviewed as if you were that person, who might be an actual person, living or dead, or a fictional character with whom your daughter is familiar.

⊙ You can be yourself and answer questions about your own real life. These might be

Materials Needed

Tape recorder (preferably hand-held, with built-in mic) and blank tape, available inexpensively at your local electronics store, OR a cell phone or other device that can record voices

questions pertaining to your current life (e.g., "What's your favorite flavor of ice cream?" "If you could have any wish, what would it be?" "Which do you like better, kisses or hugs?" "Why do you think it's so important to say 'Please' and 'Thank you'?") or questions about your past (e.g., "What was your favorite toy when you were a kid?" "Did you ever get in trouble when you were a kid? What did you do? How did your parents punish you?" "Did you have any pets when you were a kid?").

⊙ She may want to turn the tables so that you are the reporter and she is the interview subject.

Be sure to keep the recording. (You may want to transfer it to a CD, or to the hard drive of your computer, or both. In years to come, you'll love listening to your daughter as she played reporter so many years earlier.)

SCRAPBOOK NOOK

"**D**o you remember …?" Those three frequently uttered words attest to the power of memory. It's fun to remember! Remembering is even more fun when you do it together … and so is capturing the essence of today for remembering tomorrow. So gather those precious mementos and save them in a scrapbook.

Anything that's reasonably flat, such as a party invitation, photos, and perhaps a computer print-out or hand-written copy of a poem your daughter wrote, will work well. Use cardstock to mount anything that's not acid free (such as paper, magazine, or newspaper clippings) if you're interested in preserving the scrapbook for a long time. (If you enjoy scrapbooking and would like to take it to the next

Materials Needed

Scrapbook, scissors, glue, pen, patterned paper, cardstock, stickers, pictures, and flat paper souvenir materials you wish to save (photos, party invitations, newspaper clippings, postcards, movie or concert tickets, and similar memorabilia). Optional: paper trimmer (for accurate cuts)

level, there are plenty of resources out there. This is more of an informal introduction to the world of scrapbooking.)

You can also include interviews with your daughter on certain pages (e.g., What's your favorite color? What do you want to be when you grow up?). Not that the scrapbook should necessarily be about your daughter. A family-oriented scrapbook is one of the many ways to go.

Either way, you can help her select and mount in the scrapbook whatever documents she'd like to save, or you can decide together what to save, decorating the pages with patterned paper and pictures.

In pen, she can write a few words or a few sentences about the event being captured for posterity by the item that has been placed in the scrapbook, whether that's a photograph, program from her school play, or whatever else.

MOM'S EATING ALLIGATORS!

M ost license plates in most states or provinces use combinations of three or more letters along with some numerals, and those letters on those plates are all the materials you need to play Mom's Eating Alligators with your daughter the next time you're together in the car.

To play the game, simply look at the car ahead of you, or any other vehicle whose license plate you can easily read, and come up with a phrase in which the words begin with the letters on the plate. The name "Mom's Eating Alligators" comes from the first time a friend of mine played the game. My friend's sister looked at the plate of the car ahead of them, the letters on which were MEA, declared it stood for "Mom's Eating Alligators" … and thus a game was both born and named.

You and your daughter can each try to come up with

a suitably wacky phrase based on the letters on any passing plate you choose. Though you may try to top each other in goofiness, this isn't actually a competitive game. There are no winners, just fun. (Although, in a sense, you're a winner, since the game will cut down on the choruses of "Are we there yet?"!)

﹩ 5 ﹩
CREATE "FRUITFUL" STATIONERY

You and your daughter are going to create pretty stationery with fruit imprints on it by cutting one or more fruits in half (alert: this involves a sharp knife, so it may require that you cut the fruit yourself), then using the half-fruit like a rubber stamp to "stamp" the fruit

Materials Needed

One or various fruits (e.g., apple, pear, grape — nothing as uneven as a pineapple or as mushy as a plum), sharp knife, non-toxic paints, paper towel, dish, paper (preferably a pretty pastel, though white will certainly do)

19

image onto the paper.

First cut the fruit. Next fold the paper towel over at least twice and put it on the dish. Now add the paint to the paper towel, getting the towel nicely wet but not drenched. Now, holding a fruit half so that the cut side is down, wet the cut side of the fruit on the paint pad (paper towel) and apply it lightly but evenly to the top of a sheet of paper. Repeat with other sheets of paper and/or other pieces of fruit. Allow to dry. You now have fruit-themed stationery on which to write letters. Among other uses, the stationery works well for thank you notes.

⟨ 6 ⟩
ACCOUNTANT'S RACE

What do accountants do? Balance books. What does this race require you to do? Balance books … although "balance" takes on a different meaning here. You are not trying to make numbers reconcile, but rather you are *literally* "balancing" books by putting them on your heads and trying to keep them from falling off as you and your daughter compete to be the first to traverse a course … without

Materials Needed

ﷺ
Two books

dropping the books. Choose a suitable path: the length of the longest room (or hallway) in your house, or perhaps the width of your backyard.

So, each of you stands next to the other, a book balanced on your head and one on hers, and aim for the far wall, the fence, or whatever your end point is. If you drop the book, you have to stand still, reposition the book on your head, take your hand off the book, and resume walking. The fastest or most long-legged person will not necessarily be the winner.

On your mark, get set, go!

ৡ 7 ৶
GEOGRAPHY

This is not a game for your four-year-old daughter but rather for your eight-year-old daughter (or older). It requires some knowledge of place names and what letter each starts with. If you lead the game off — by naming any place name you choose — and you start with "Mississippi," then, since your place name ended in an "I," your daughter now has to name a place that starts with an "I." "Iceland," she says, and it's a "D" back to you.

Should you pick "Denmark" or "Denver" or "Dubuque"? Depends on which one you think she'll have a

Materials Needed

None

comeback for. If you say "Denmark," she has to name a place beginning with "K" ("Kentucky"? "Kansas"? "Kenya"?). Can she think of one *that hasn't been used already in this game?* Because if it has, nobody can use it again.

The first player who can't think of a place name beginning with the requisite letter that hasn't been used before is out of the game … and the other player wins.

) 8 (
FLOWERED HAIR CLIPS

*U*sing the glue gun will probably fall to you, Mom, unless your daughter is old enough to use one responsibly, but designing the hair clip is definitely her part of this fun activity. Let her design each clip, placing the flower(s) and faux gemstone(s) where she wants them in relation to each other as they will be when affixed to the

Materials Needed

Silver-colored hair clips, plastic flowers, rhinestones or other imitation gems, glue gun

clip. Then you can use the glue gun to fasten each decorative item in place as selected by your daughter.

Not only can she wear the clips she creates, but she can also give them as gifts to her friends.

❧ 9 ❧
PROGRESSIVE STORIES – NON-ALPHABETICAL

P rogressive Stories is a fun game that requires nothing but imagination. The first time you play this with your daughter, it will probably be best if you begin the game. Do so by starting a story … any fictional story, which can be about a little girl, or a dragon, or a family, or a cat — you choose who the story's going to be about, and make it up as you go along.

And you'll go along for perhaps the spoken equivalent of a paragraph or three at the most. Then, just at a

Materials Needed

None

crucial moment, you'll stop the story. What defines a crucial moment? It could be that the little girl found a shoebox on the sidewalk, but when she took off the lid, inside she saw not a pair of shoes but _____. Or it could be that the twin sisters discovered a secret door in the attic, and when the door slowly creaked open, they were amazed by the sight of a _____! Or that the dragon was lonely because no one wanted to play with him. And then, one day, something amazing happened ...

So you'll stop the story after just a short while, at some sort of cliffhanger point, and now it will be your daughter's turn to take up the story and tell it. She, too, should keep the narrative short before turning the story back over to you, preferably (though not absolutely essentially) at another cliffhanger point.

And so the story goes, switching back and forth from player to player, with each player adding on to what has gone before. The game ends when someone brings the story to a satisfactory conclusion, or when everyone agrees that they have had enough and want to do something else.

❧ 10 ❧
PROGRESSIVE STORIES – ALPHABETICAL

Quite similar to the game in the previous entry, this version is for older players who want more of a challenge to their story-telling prowess and who know the alphabet and how to spell. In this version, each player's contribution to the story is just one sentence long at a time, and the sentences must follow in alphabetical order. That is, the player who starts the story does so with just one sentence, which can begin with any letter of the alphabet. Let's say your opening sentence is, "One day, a little girl named Jenny decided she wanted to visit her grandma." Your daughter's first contribution to the story must be one sentence long also, and it must start with the next letter of the alphabet after the one that started your sentence. Since your sentence began with an "O," your daughter's sentence must start with a "P." Then it's back to you for another addition to the story: a sentence starting with "Q."

Note: It is permissible, when playing this game, to agree in advance to omit certain letters of the alphabet. The usual candidates for omission are Q, X, and Z, though that's not a rule you need to feel bound by.

Another note: In this version of the game, even more than in the non-alphabetic version, it is common for the setting, plot, and even the protagonist of the story to change ... perhaps several times during the course of the story. Keep in mind that this is not "against the rules," nor is there any reason for you to discourage such switches. The only rules that need to be adhered to are that each story contribution be one sentence long, and that the sentences proceed in alphabetical order.

As with the "Progressive Stories" earlier in the book, the game is over when the story comes to a logical conclusion or when the players tire of it ... or, in this case, you may decide that the story is to end when you have come back to the letter of the alphabet with which you led off the game.

❧ 11 ❧

LICK-IT-STICK-IT GLUE

Be warned: Here's some good messy fun your daughter can get into — and the result will be glue she can actually use (for pasting pictures or photos or other items into scrapbooks, for pasting construction-paper cut-outs onto other pieces of construction paper, and for any other projects she'd normally use paste or glue for … such as the scrapbooking activity on page 16). Here's how to make the glue. Your help will definitely be needed.

Heat the water in a saucepan and pour the gelatin into the bowl. When

Materials Needed

1/4-ounce packet of unflavored gelatin, 1/4 cup of boiling water, one tablespoon of sugar, saucepan, fork, heatproof bowl, storage container (optional — needed only if you don't use all of the adhesive immediately)

the water is boiling, pour it over the gelatin and stir the mixture with the fork until the gelatin is dissolved. Now add the sugar, and stir until the sugar is fully dissolved. Allow it to cool and firm up before licking.

Besides the uses listed above, your daughter can use the glue to stick pretend stamps on envelopes, and to stick homemade stickers onto stationery. If she doesn't use it right away, the glue will dry; she can wet the glue to re-moisten it when she's ready to use it.

⸙ 12 ⸙
STICK PUPPETS

Your young puppeteer is going to present a show ... after she creates the very simple, basic puppets she needs. To fashion the puppets, she needs to either cut pictures of people out of magazines or draw them herself on construction paper, using crayons. And your part in this activity? You're going to help and work alongside her.

Search together for magazine pictures of people.

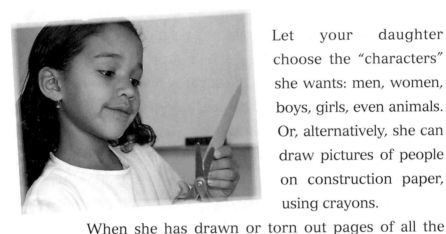

Let your daughter choose the "characters" she wants: men, women, boys, girls, even animals. Or, alternatively, she can draw pictures of people on construction paper, using crayons.

When she has drawn or torn out pages of all the pictures of people she wants for her puppet theatre (five or so is plenty), she needs to cut around the pictures so that all background is removed and just the figure of the person (or animal) is left. (You can help her with this if she's too young to do it properly on her own.) Then she needs to glue or paste the picture to a Popsicle stick.

She can script a play if she wants, though she's more likely to be interested in impromptu dialogue. Either way, she can turn a small table on its side and get down behind the top (now the front) of the table, hold the

Materials Needed

Pictures of people cut from magazines or drawn by your daughter on construction paper, crayons (if using the construction paper option), scissors, paste or glue, Popsicle sticks, card table lying on its side or dining room table or other suitable "puppet theater"

puppets so that her hands are below the tabletop but the puppets are above it, and put on a show for you. Or, lacking a small table, she can crouch on the far side of the dining room table and hold the puppets just above the table surface.

Don't forget to applaud! Every showperson needs an appreciative audience.

꒰ 13 ꒱

SALT-AND-FLOUR BEADS

*Y*our daughter can make jewelry to wear herself or give as gifts. She can also make beaded jewelry ... and the best part is, she gets to make the beads herself! Here's how:

In a bowl, mix the salt and flour, and add enough water that the mixture has a doughy consistency. If you want, add a few drops of food coloring. (If you want more than one color of beads, get one or more additional bowls, separate the dough, putting some in each bowl, and add a different color of food coloring to each bowl.)

Two cups of table salt, one cup of flour, water, food coloring or paint (acrylic or tempera), bowl, toothpick, newspaper to work on, thin string or dental floss, paintbrush (if you are using paint rather than food coloring), measuring cup

If you don't dye the beads with food coloring in the "dough" stage, you will be painting them on the outside after they are formed and dried. Painting them afterward produces more bright and diverse colors, but dyeing the "dough" from which you make the beads is quicker and less messy.

Now form small pieces of the mixture into beads. Pierce each bead with a toothpick all the way through, remove the toothpick, and leave the bead to dry.

When all the beads are dried, if you didn't color them with food coloring, paint them with tempera or acrylic paint. You will need to paint one side at a time, let it dry, then paint the other side.

String the beads into one or more necklaces or bracelets.

∮ 14 ∮
ALPHABET ON WHEELS

If your daughter enjoys playing Alphabet House (see page 92), introduce her to Alphabet on Wheels during your next car trip.

She plays by looking out the car window for the various letters of the alphabet, "A," "B," and so forth, which she may find on billboards, street signs, speed limit signs, license plates, or, if you're in town rather than on the highway, on the storefronts you pass. But — here's the catch that keeps the game from being too easy and ending too quickly — she has to look for the letters *in order.* That is, she must first find an "A" before she looks for a "B." So if that hard-to-find "X" pops up on a storefront before she's found "W," it's no use. She can't claim it yet (or "store" it for future use).

Materials Needed

None

More challenging variation: For a greater challenge, make it a rule that the letter in question has to *begin* the word (or be in the first position on a license plate).

Another variation: Have your daughter look not for

the actual letters but for objects that are spelled *beginning with* the letter she is seeking. That is, for "C" she needs to spot an object that is spelled beginning with a "C" — like "car." (That was an easy one … but what will she do for "X" and "Z" — unless you drive past the zoo?)

∿ 15 ∿

BUTTERFLY SAFARI

Take your daughter out to "capture" some of nature's brightest beauties … with your camera. It doesn't need to be a digital camera, though it surely can be. (A cell phone camera will work too — anything that can take a picture of the butterflies you encounter on your "safari.") Clearly this is a warm-weather activity, when the most butterflies are around.

If you've used a digital camera, you can begin the second part of your safari as soon as you return home.

Materials Needed

Camera, book about butterflies and/or encyclopedia and/or computer (to look up butterflies on the Web)

When you have the pictures in front of you, the second phase of your hunt begins: a quest for information.

Daughters old enough to read can peruse a butterfly book (perhaps borrowed from the library), the encyclopedia, or the Web right along with you. Daughters below reading age, or those just learning to sound out C-A-T will need to rely on you to look up the facts and read them aloud. Either way, you can both work together on finding a picture in the book or on the Web that matches up to the photo of each butterfly you "captured," so that you can identify the species by name, then read up to learn more about it.

♪ 16 ♪
BUBBLING FOUNTAIN

This is another just-for-fun project that offers double your fun, both in making the mixture and then in watching the results as the bubble erupts like a fountain or geyser. Here's how you and your daughter can create a bubbling fountain together:

Be sure to work in a sink or tub, or outdoors — somewhere where the overflow and any spillage will not harm anyone or anything. Now, first put the neck of the funnel into the bottle. Then add the water, baking soda, and detergent through the funnel into the bottle. Last, pour the vinegar through the funnel into the bottle. Immediately remove the funnel and let go of the bottle. Stand back, so nobody gets sprayed.

Now watch the bottle bubble and "erupt."

Materials Needed

Two cups of water, one tablespoon of baking soda, a few drops of liquid detergent, three tablespoons of vinegar, tall bottle with a narrow neck (such as a soda bottle), funnel, measuring cup, measuring spoons

ᘑ 17 ᘒ

BREAD-DOUGH CLAY

Think how much more fun it is for your daughter to work in clay when she's made it herself ... with Mommy's help, of course. Want to know how? Okay!

Remove the crusts from the bread. (You do not need a knife. It can be done by hand.) Tear the bread into small pieces — perhaps 1/2" squares. (It does not need to be exact.) Place them in the bowl. Add the glue and lemon juice to the bread and mush it and squeeze it together with your fingers till it no longer resembles bread and has a uniform consistency. This is your bread-dough clay.

Materials Needed

Four slices of white bread, three tablespoons of white glue, two drops of lemon juice, paint, bowl, paintbrush, plastic bag for storing leftover clay, measuring spoons

Now that she has made her clay, your daughter (and you, too!) can form the clay mixture into animals, flowers, or whatever else you two want. You'll need to leave your creations out to dry for one or two days (depending on the humidity). Meanwhile, store the excess mixture in the plastic bag, in the refrigerator, to play with another day. And when your creations are dry, paint them.

꒰ 18 ꒱

PERFUME, INC.

Making your own perfume — what fun! Your daughter will delight in creating a floral scent that she can wear — and perhaps you'll choose to wear some of it too.

First go out together to pick some flowers. Make sure your daughter knows where it's okay to pick flowers (e.g., flowers that grow in your yard or grow wild), and where it isn't (e.g., flowers that grow in your neighbor's garden). Also caution her about thorns if necessary. You can also buy inexpensive fragrant flowers (e.g., carnations) at the florist's or supermarket. Whether you pick them or buy them, choose fragrant ones. Looks are unimportant. You can pick just one kind, or several different kinds, from which to create your perfume.

Once you're back home with your flowers, cut them into pieces, then mash them with the mortar and pestle, or, alternatively, with the back of a spoon against a bowl. *If you have collected more than one kind of flower, keep the different types separate from each other.* Mash up one kind in one bowl, another type in another bowl.

Now process each kind of flower separately in the following way: Line the sieve or funnel or coffee filter basket with tissue paper, white paper towel, or a paper coffee filter. Place the mashed-up flowers of one kind into the lined container and pour a little hot tap water through it while you hold it over the bowl. How much water you use will depend on how many crushed flowers you have, but start with perhaps 1/8 cup or even less.

Materials Needed

Some pretty-smelling flowers, hot water from the tap, either a mortar and pestle or the back of a spoon and a bowl or something similar to crush the flowers with, tissue paper, white paper towel or paper coffee filters, a funnel or a sieve or a coffee filter basket, bowl; small, clean, preferably glass containers (one for each kind of flower you have picked — baby food jars are good for this, or olive jars, or something similar); eyedropper, paper and pen or pencil (optional)

When the water is finished straining, you will be left with wet, mashed-up flowers in the sieve, strainer, or coffee filter basket. Discard those. You will also be left with the water, which now smells of the flowers and is properly called essence (rose essence, violet essence, jasmine essence, honeysuckle essence, etc.). Pour this into one clean jar. Repeat this process for each kind of flower you have collected and crushed up.

If you have been working with only one kind of flower — say, roses — you now have rose essence, which is your perfume. But most perfumes are blended of different kinds of essences. And that's what you can do now. If you have two, three, five, or any number of different essences, your daughter can now combine them in different ways to make different perfumes. The best way is using an eyedropper.

She might want to keep track of the different formulas she creates. If she finds that four drops of rose essence, two drops of violet essence, and one drop of honeysuckle essence create a perfume she particularly likes, she may want to re-create the formula again some other time. So writing down the formulas isn't a bad idea.

She can blend different mixtures, giving each one a name just like perfume companies do. She can even make different perfumes for each of her friends, creating an individual scent for each friend she gives a small bottle of fragrance to, so each one is special for that friend.

And of course, she can give you a bottle of her special perfume too!

≥ 19 ≤

INVISIBLE INK

If your daughter is old enough to read and write, she's old enough for secret messages written in invisible ink. You can leave these secret messages for each other, with the content being anything from "I love you" to "There's a treat hidden in the silverware drawer for you" to "Tonight is spaghetti night!" Here's how you write (and read) a message in invisible ink:

Squeeze or otherwise juice the lemon, and pour the

Materials Needed

☗

Lemon juice,
toothpick, heat
source such as a
radiator, lemon
squeezer or citrus
juicer, bowl or
cup, paper

juice into the bowl or cup. Dip the toothpick into the lemon juice and use it like a pen to write on the paper. When the juice dries, it will be invisible. Now give the note to your daughter. (Or have her write a message and give it to you.) You or she can make your "invisible ink" messages reappear by holding the paper over or under a heat source (such as a radiator).

♪ 20 ♪

RHYTHM BAND

Whether or not your daughter aspires to be a drummer in a band when she grows up, she (and you!) can have fun playing homemade (or toy) "percussion instruments" now. Anything that makes noise when you beat or bang on it can be considered — at least for these purposes — a percussion instrument ... though I wouldn't suggest you use anything valuable, of course. In fact, the possibilities are fairly limitless. Or at least, they're limited only by what you have around the house, whether it's breakable, and whether the noise level it will create is more than you can tolerate. Toy percussion instruments, such as drums or tambourines, are also fine for this activity.

Select your "instruments" — yes, plural … one for you, too, Mom. And decide whether you are going to accompany yourselves as you sing or provide additional percussion for background music. Then put on the music, or start singing … and help your daughter try to learn how to keep in rhythm with the music.

Materials Needed

Whatever will create a good noisy percussion accompaniment to music, such as a metal pot and a wooden spoon, or a toy drum or tambourine, or even just a large, thick piece of cardboard to beat time on

⸹ 21 ⸺

LOCOMOTION COMMOTION

I n these days of "programmed exercise," people jog, lift weights, do yoga, ride bikes ... but not enough people walk unless they are going from point A to point B.

Whatever happened to walking just for fun?

Or perhaps you could even walk for a cause — you know, the sort of fund-raiser in which you get people to pledge a certain amount of money for

Materials Needed

None

each mile you walk, to be donated to a cause that's dear to your heart, or to your daughter's. (If she's really little, she may not understand walking for a cause or the whole concept of charitable organizations, but if she's a bit older, she may be interested in a certain cause.)

If you walk for a cause, your daughter gets a quintuple benefit:

1❖ She learns about working to help worthy causes.

2❖ She gets to help the organization of her choice.

3❖ She gets to spend some meaningful and special time with you.

4❖ She gets good exercise.

5❖ The walk itself can be enjoyable in other ways, too: When you walk, you get to see far more of your surroundings than you do when those surroundings zip past you in a moving car. You can also stop to pick a flower, gather acorns, smell the tomatoes growing in a garden on the other side of the fence, watch birds, observe cloud shapes ("What does that cloud remind you of?"), and generally interact with your surroundings — if not physically, then intellectually (observing your surroundings, asking questions, even guessing at the stories behind what you observe).

Your car *can* be a part of your excursions, though: Instead of walking around the same old block every time, or always walking the same two-mile stretch of roads or city streets, you can drive to different neighborhoods and then walk around them.

♪ 22 ♪

GOOFY GOLF

Even if you've never held a golf club, you and your daughter can play Goofy Golf together. And you don't have to dig up the yard to play!

In Goofy Golf, you score not by sinking a ball in a hole but by driving it between a pair of blocks (or any other suitable objects that serve as markers for the "goal" at which you aim the ball). And the "ball" isn't a regulation golf ball at all; it's a pair or three of mismatched socks, rolled up. For that matter, the golf club isn't a real golf club either; it's a newspaper bat, made of rolled-up newspapers. You can share a newspaper bat or make one for each of you.

To make a newspaper bat, roll some newspapers together tightly and tape them together. Make the newspaper bat long enough to reach from the player's hands to the ground, and

Materials Needed

Two newspaper bats (for which you need several sections of newspaper and some tape), sock ball (for which you need several mismatched socks — now there's a use for them!), blocks or any other suitable objects with which to delineate "goals" to drive the balls through

thick enough that it won't crumple when it connects with the sock ball (or with a rock in the grass).

A Goofy Golf course doesn't have to have the regulation nine or eighteen holes — it can be any number that works for you, depending on the size of your playing area and the number of blocks (or other goal delineators) you have at your disposal. You can even play a regulation nine-hole game by setting up three holes and ruling that one game consists of hitting the ball through each of the three holes, then going around again, and then again ... for a total of nine.

Delineate a tee for each hole — the spot where you'll each place your sock ball to tee off. Now keep track of how many strokes it takes each player to hit the sock ball through each pair of markers ("into each hole"). As in any golf game, of course, the winner is the player who gets around the course with the lowest score.

If a ball goes beyond the hole without passing between the markers, the player needs to swat it back and try again. A hole is scored when the ball passes between the markers, going in the right direction. A ball that lands in a "hazard" (flower bed or other unplayable spot) can be dropped at the edge of the hazard nearest where it went in, with the player taking a two-stroke penalty.

∿ 23 ∿
SCRATCH "PAINTINGS"

*Y*ou and your daughter can each work on one of these at the same table, comparing your results when you're finished. First, cover all of the paper with random stripes and swirls and swoops and segments of different colors of watercolor paint. (Do not use black paint.) You don't need to attempt to form a pattern, draw a picture, or be at all artistic. Random coloring is what's called for. Just be sure you cover the entire page with color.

When the page is covered in color and the paint has dried, take the black crayon and cover every drop of color you've just applied. When the paper is totally black, use the edge of a coin to lightly scratch lines and swirls through the black crayon. As the black covering is scratched away, colorful lines will appear on the uniform blackness of

Materials Needed

Paper (ordinary typing paper will do, but heavier paper such as construction paper is preferable), watercolor paints and brushes, two black crayons, two coins of any denomination (one for each of you), newspaper to cover your work surface

the page. You won't know in advance just what colors you're going to reveal. All the randomness of the original coloring, beneath the equally random swoops of coin-scratch, result in wildly unusual shifts in shade and tone.

Compare your results afterward. (But remember that this is *not* a contest to see who has the prettiest, most colorful, or most unusual picture.)

₰ 24 ₰

RECYCLED PAPER

I t's never too early for kids to learn how to reduce, reuse, and recycle. Does your daughter have any idea how paper is made? What about recycled paper? She's going to recycle some newspaper and turn it into paper in this fun experiment that will require more or less of your help, depending on your daughter's age. Here's how the two of you go about making recycled paper:

Cut the bottoms out of the two identical plastic containers so that each cutout forms a rectangle the size of the paper you want to wind up with. Place the two pieces of wire screening between the two boxes, and put the whole thing in the sink. Fill the blender two-thirds of the way with lukewarm water. Now drop the ten torn strips of newsprint into the blender, while the blender whirrs on a low setting.

Pour the contents of the blender onto the top screen of your contraption in the sink. Let the water drain through into the sink, leaving behind a pulpy product, which will remain on the screen. When the water is pretty well drained out, take off the top container, which will give you access to the top screen and the pulp.

Lift the top screen and pulp carefully out and set it on the counter. This exposes the second screen. Place it on the top of the pulp. Cover it with the plastic bag, and roll across the bag with the rolling pin. Remove the bag. Leave the screens. Place the dishtowel over the pulp, and place the heavy-weighted object over it.

Leave it for a day or two or three, checking it for dryness. When it's dry, you'll have recycled paper that you've made yourself.

❧ 25 ❧

SILLY SHORT STORIES

This game can be played by two, three, or six players (with slight changes in the rules). I'm going to give you the rules for a two-person game, assuming the players are only you and your daughter.

The two of you are going to write what amounts to a short, and probably amusing, story. No player will know what any other player has written until the game is over, which takes six moves.

One long piece of paper (at least 8.5" x 11"), pen or pencil, preferably one for each player

Let's assume you go first. At the top of the piece of paper, write down the name of any female — real or fictional, living or dead, adult or child, or even a fictional animal with human characteristics, like Daisy Duck. It must, however, be a name that's recognizable to both players. It could be Mrs. McGillicuddy, the music teacher with the huge glasses. It could be Minnie Mouse. It could be Barbie, as in Barbie Dolls, or Brittany, your daughter's best friend, or Nana, or even your daughter herself. Write the name in small letters, right at the top of the page, then fold the page over just far enough that your daughter can't see whose name you've written, and hand it to your daughter.

Conscientiously keeping the paper folded, and having no idea who the named female is, your daughter writes "met" and the name of a male — again real or fictional, living or dead, adult or child, person or anthropomorphic animal — as long as it's a name recognizable to both of the players. Then she folds the paper again and hands it back to you.

You write "at" or "in" or conceivably even "on,"

followed by a place: "at the school dance," "on Saturn," "in a movie studio in Hollywood," "in the bathtub" — some location recognizable to all players. Then you fold the paper over once again, returning it to your daughter.

Now, remember, she knows only the identity of the male involved, not the female. It is her responsibility now to write "She said," followed by a quotation: "Did you do your homework?" "Want to dance?" "I hate brussels sprouts," "Peace on Earth," "Cowabunga," "What time is the party?" "Meow." Then she folds the paper again.

Back to you. You write down, "He said," followed by a statement or question, again without knowing who the "he" in question is: "I said no!" "What was the question?" "Marry me! Marry me!" "It's great weather for tennis," "I'm gonna tell your mother." "Ouch! I got a bee sting." Then the paper gets folded one last time, and passed again.

And back to your daughter, who writes, "So they," followed by an action: "got a divorce," "had dinner," "had seventeen kids," "dug up worms for bait," "scored seven touchdowns in the first half," "put out the fire," "got on *American Idol*."

The paper is passed back to you for one last time —

not to write anything on, this time, but to read. Unfurl the paper and read aloud the story that has just been cobbled together by you two underinformed collaborators. The results are unpredictable at least, hysterical at best.

Next time, let your daughter start the game, with you going second, so you both get a chance to supply each part of the "story."

❧ 26 ❧
GROW AN HERB GARDEN

Cooking is so much more fun when you've grown some of the ingredients yourself. This activity starts with a trip to your local gardening center. (Include your daughter on this outing as well as in the plant maintenance thereafter.) Once there, inquire as to what herbs and/or veggies are easy to grow in a window box, and then buy everything you need (see the material list, at right), unless you already have some of

Materials Needed

Small window boxes, soil, seeds or cuttings, and possibly fertilizer

the needed materials at home. If you're not knowledgeable about gardening, get instructions too.

Now it's back home to plant the seeds or seedlings, water them, and tend to them daily thereafter (or however frequently you've been advised to water and other-wise care for them). Whatever you do — pruning, transplant-ing, fertilizing — to care for your veggies/herbs, do it together.

Invite your daughter to be the one to snip off the dill, oregano, sage, or whatever herb you need for each night's dinner. And if you've planted veggies, she may even take a bite or two of ones she has formerly shunned. Funny how things taste better when you grow them yourself!

CROSS-LEGGED RACE

In this non-traditional cross-legged race, you and your daughter must race with one leg crossed in front of the other. If you uncross your legs at any point, you forfeit the race and the other player wins automatically. It's not easy! But it will be easier for your daughter than it will be for you.

Find an area in which you can both race side by side and cover a distance of preferably at least ten feet. Delineate the start and finish lines either by chalking the sidewalk, driveway, or concrete basement floor, or by laying two lengths of string down on a carpeted or tiled floor indoors. When each player reaches the finish line, she turns around — *still with her legs crossed* — and races back to the start line. It is the first player who returns to the start line without uncrossing her legs at any point who wins the race.

Ready? Set? Go!

Materials Needed

None

❧ 28 ❧

CREATE A FAMILY FLAG

Working together, design a family flag. It should not only reflect your tastes but also something about the family. You might have four stars for the four family members, or a circle because your family's interests are well rounded, or a pine tree because your house is

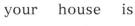

Materials Needed

Heavyweight paper and markers, and (optional) material and a sewing machine

surrounded by pine trees, or a starfish because you live near the sea, or it could have the family motto on it, if you have one.

After you have agreed in principle on the design, draw it on both sides of a piece of heavyweight paper, using marking pens.

After that, if you want, you and/or your daughter can get some heavyweight material, get out the sewing machine, and create a real flag along the same design.

Fly your family's flag proudly.

≀ 29 ≀

DUCK-WALK RACE

S urely you remember duck-walking when you were a kid. Crouch down, grab your ankles, and waddle. Easy then. Not so easy now. Which is why this is yet another race that your daughter has a fair chance of winning.

Everything I said about laying out the field for the Cross-Legged Race (see page 56) applies here: where to run it, how to lay out the start and finish lines, and the fact that rough concrete can't be totally ignored since either player (and more likely you!) may well lose her balance and fall.

Materials Needed

None

You may choose to run/waddle to the finish line and back to the start again, or to end the race at the finish line.

May the best duck win!

Variation: Cross-handed duck-walk: Instead of grasping the left ankle with the left hand and the right ankle with the right hand, each player grasps the left ankle with the right hand and the right ankle with the left hand. This makes movement very difficult and very slow. It also makes watching the race as much fun as participating.

❧ 30 ❧

COW-A-PLASTIC

*Y*ou and your daughter are going to "cook" a batch of fantastic elastic plastic … and it's even more fantastic because it's made out of *milk*! If you're all set for the next fun kitchen experiment, here's how you go about creating Cow-a-Plastic:

Pour the milk into the saucepan and heat it over medium-high heat till lumps form in the milk. Now hold the saucepan over the sink, and slowly and carefully pour the liquid into the sink so that the lumpy stuff remains in the saucepan. Use the spoon to lift the lumps out of the saucepan and place them in the jar. Now add the vinegar to the jar, and let the whole thing sit there for at least an hour. At that point, the jar will have in it a rubbery blob and some more liquid. Pour this liquid down the sink drain and remove the rubbery blob.

Shape the rubbery blob into a ball, and leave it on the paper towel to dry for at least a few hours. You have made a plastic ball you can play with (roll it or throw it — don't bounce it). Your daughter can also paint it with acrylic paints and keep it to decorate her dresser, night table, or desk.

Materials Needed

Four ounces of milk, one teaspoon of vinegar, one small saucepan, one small clean jar, one spoon, one folded-over piece of paper towel

◊ 31 ◊
TREASURE HUNT

There are two ways to conduct a treasure hunt … or you can combine the two.

⊙ You can draw a map that's simple enough for your daughter to follow but not so simple that she'll take one look at it and beeline right to the treasure.

⊙ If she's old enough to read reasonably well, you can leave her a series of notes, each one leading to the location of the next note till the final note points her to the location of the treasure.

⊙ You can give her a map that leads to the location of the first note, and from there she follows one note to the next to the next … and ultimately to the treasure.

The notes should be somewhat cryptic. Don't be so plainspoken as to say, "Look at the base of the tree in the backyard." But don't be so cryptic as to utterly confound her and leave her frustrated so that the game is no fun,

Materials Needed

A "treasure" to hide, a map you have drawn and/or pieces of paper on which you have written clues

61

and/or so that she gives up. If you want to point her to the base of the oak tree, and she has a swing set right next to it, your clue might read, "Swing high, swing low, and look down."

How many notes she will have to find depends on:

⊙ How old (and how patient) she is, and how well she reads

⊙ How many good hiding places there are in your house

⊙ How much time you want the game to take

And the treasure? It could be her favorite treat, a note that says "I.O.U. one ice cream," a small and inexpensive toy, a piece of play jewelry, or actual money for your daughter's piggy bank.

∤ 32 ∤
WHAT'S MISSING?

Test your daughter's powers of observation with this fun game, which is based on Rudyard Kipling's book *Kim's Game*. Prepare for the game in advance by placing ten small objects on a tray, a platter, a very large plate, or some similar large, flat surface that can be carried into and out of the room. Suitable objects might include a penny, a thimble, a safety pin, a pen, a nail file, a golf tee, a spoon, a button, a paper clip, and a rubber band ... or any assortment of ten items you have around the house that are reasonably familiar to your daughter. (Do not use anything she will not recognize immediately or does not know the name for.)

Give her a minute or so to study the objects on the tray, then take the tray out of the room (out of your daughter's sight) and remove any one of the objects. Now return to the room with the tray, show it to her, and ask her what's missing.

If your daughter is very young,

Materials Needed

꙳

Tray, platter, or similar; ten assorted small items

you may want to place only five items on the tray initially, removing one to leave just four.

If your daughter is significantly older, you can make the challenge more difficult by using more than ten items, and/or by making the items deliberately and confusingly similar: three coins of different denominations, a needle and a pin, buttons of three different colors. Or another way to make the game more challenging for an older girl is to rearrange the order of the remaining nine objects after you remove one of them. In addition to removing one item, you can also add one, so that you still have ten items, but only nine of the original ones. Now your daughter needs to tell you both what's missing and what has been added.

This is a great game for birthday parties!

﹩ 33 ﹫

MOCK STAINED GLASS PICTURES

Crumple the foil so it wrinkles, and then use it to cover the cardboard, and tape it in place. Secure the plastic wrap to your table or desktop with tape. Using black marker, outline on the plastic wrap a design of your choice; then fill it in with colored marker. When the picture is completed, lift up the wrap and tape it carefully over the foil.

Some designs seem especially suited to this activity — for example, colorful holiday designs, bright spring flowers, and autumn cornucopias.

Materials Needed

Small piece of lightweight cardboard (such as the backing from a legal notepad), piece of aluminum foil a couple of inches larger than the cardboard, plastic wrap cut slightly larger than the foil, tape, black and colored markers

》 34 《

NEW CRAYONS FROM OLD

*Y*our daughter will definitely need your help with this activity as it involves using the oven. You're going to be melting down the stubs of old crayons and blending them with other old crayon stubs to form new, larger crayons in new shades and hues.

Here's what you do: Preheat your oven to 200°. While the oven heats, remove the paper from all your crayon stubs. Now separate all the crayon stubs into color families. One good way to group them is:

⊙ Blues and purples

⊙ Greens

⊙ Reds and pinks

⊙ Yellows and oranges

⊙ Earth tones and other neutrals

Count the number of groups (color families) you have. (I've listed five, but you may not have crayons in all five color families; you might, for example, have blues and purples, reds and pinks, and earth tones and other neutrals but no stubs of yellows

Materials Needed

Stubs of old crayons, one whole crayon, cookie sheet, aluminum foil, pot holders

and oranges, or of greens.)

Now create one "form" for each group you have. To do this, first wrap a double layer of aluminum foil, approximately the length of a whole, new crayon, slightly more than halfway around a crayon. You need just enough folded-over foil to wrap partway around the crayon — a little more than halfway surround-

ing it. Now remove the crayon. You have just made a form. Do this once for each color family you have. (If you have only shades of red and shades of blue — two color families — you will need two forms. If you also have yellows and oranges, you will need three forms. For shades of brown, you will need another form. And so on.) Next, put all the stubs from each color family into one form. You can put one behind another in the semi-cylindrical form, till you run out of stubs from that color family or fill up the form. (If you have a lot of stubs, or several really large ones, split them up into two forms. They may not all fit in one.)

Crimp both ends of each form after you have filled it

with the stubs. This is so that when the crayon stubs melt, the melted crayons don't ooze out of the forms. Line a cookie sheet with aluminum foil and lay the forms onto the lined cookie sheet. (Now you have extra protection against any possible leakage.)

Place the whole thing in the preheated oven. After about ten minutes, peek to make sure the crayon stubs all look well melted together; and if they do, remove the cookie sheet. Allow your new crayons to cool and solidify for around half an hour before you remove them from the forms. The crayons won't be perfectly rounded and smooth but will be very intriguing colors.

Note: You can also mix two color families in one form. The blue family and the red family will give you a purple crayon, for instance. But don't mix more than two color families, or you'll wind up with a very unattractive color as a result.

$ 35 {

POMANDER BALLS

omander balls are fun to make and fragrant to smell at any time of the year. Since apples and oranges are available year-round at the super-market, there's no reason to confine this activity to the holiday season.

Just stick the cloves into the apples or oranges, about 1/4" apart, then wrap each piece of fruit separately in netting. Gather the netting and tie it at the top with the yarn, with a loop left in the yarn for hanging. You can now hang your pomander ball in a closet or in an open area of a room to add a sweet/sharp fresh scent.

Materials Needed

Apples or oranges, whole cloves, netting, yarn

ᛐ 36 ᛑ
MOBILES

*Y*ou can work on one mobile together (recommended if your daughter is younger) or you can each work on your own mobile. Here's how: First, cut out the people or animals from some photos or, alternatively, find interesting and colorful magazine pictures, cut around them carefully, and paste one to both sides of each piece of cardboard. (Alternatively you can cut shapes out of the cardboard: stars, circles, trees, houses, dogs, crescent moons, or people. Color each shape on both sides.)

Materials Needed

Nylon thread, supports such as rods and/or hangers, scissors, glue or paste, cardboard, magazines and/or photos; crayons or markers (optional)

A really simple mobile might consist merely of a hanger with nylon thread suspended from each end and a cardboard cut-out picture hanging from each piece of nylon thread. Multi-level mobiles are trickier but more fun. You can hang a wire hanger or a rod from each end of another hanger or a larger rod, with a cardboard picture hanging from each end of each rod. How many tiers you construct will depend on your patience and your skill in balancing objects to keep the mobile from tipping.

Hang the mobiles from plant hooks fixed into the ceiling, or in any other spot in your house that seems suitable and affords a place to hang them from.

37

GUESS WHO I AM!

Here is a mildly competitive guessing game, in which each round can have a winner, though there may not be a winner at all. The first person to play — let's say it's you, Mom — thinks of a person the other person would also be able to identify. This person may be fictional or real, living or dead, and male or female, and some allow animals as well as people, so that Bugs Bunny, Winnie the Pooh, or your family's dog are also fair game. (Decide in advance if you will allow animals or not.) In other words, you might choose George

Materials Needed

None

Washington, Grandma, Wonder Woman, Elmo from Sesame Street, or the girl who lives next door.

Now your daughter gets twenty yes-or-no questions to figure out who that person is. Logical questions to start with are, "Are you a real person?" "Are you alive now?" "Are you female?" "Are you an animal?" (Obviously if the answer is "No" to "Are you a real person?" you would not ask "Are you alive now?")

Some of the follow-up questions might be, "Have I ever talked to you?" "Do you live around here?" "Were you at my birthday party?" "Are you famous?"

If your daughter can guess "who you are" in twenty questions, she wins. Whether she wins or not, she now gets to decide on an identity while it's your turn to guess "who she is." You can agree in advance to play a certain number of rounds, and tally up the number of times each of you won, to pick a grand winner of the game, or you can just play each round for its own sake, winning or not, as the case may be.

♪ 38 ♪

PICNIC PARADISE

Your family may enjoy backyard barbeques in warm weather, but when's the last time you had a picnic? This one's going to be a mother-daughter affair: just the two of you.

Plan a menu that your daughter can help prepare. It can be simply peanut butter and jelly sandwiches or something more elaborate.

Choose foods that:

⊙ she can help prepare;

⊙ you both like to eat;

⊙ transport well without going bad or getting soggy or suffering other mishaps.

Also bring along an activity — something you can do together at the picnic site. This may be your hula hoops (see page 107), a ball to play catch with, your knitting (see page 125), two books of word puzzles (one for each of you), or any other toy, game, or activity that's easy to transport and is suited to

Materials Needed

Homemade lunch, napkins and any needed utensils, and a fun activity to enjoy while you're outside

outdoor enjoyment.

Where are you going to have your picnic? You can choose a nearby public park, or one farther away that you haven't ever been to (or at least don't visit often), your local zoo (if they allow picnics and have a picnic area), or even your own backyard. Or choose some other venue.

After you've prepared your picnic lunch together and walked, driven, or biked to the picnic site, have lunch, play games, and indulge in some heart-to-heart mother/daughter conversation. Now would be a good time to tell your daughter why you're proud of her, or what the three best things about her are, or some other positive reinforcement. And if she has anything serious on her mind, encourage her to talk about it while you listen and respond thoughtfully.

You can make these picnics a regular occurrence (at least in good weather) or a once-in-a-blue-moon special occasion.

❧ 39 ❧

SOAP BUBBLE SOLUTION

Help your daughter make her own bubble liquid with which to blow soap bubbles. Here's how:

Put the dishwashing liquid, water, and glycerine in the bowl and stir well. That's all! You now have your own soap bubble solution — in large quantity — and your daughter can proudly proclaim, "We made it ourselves!"

As for blowing the bubbles, you can use a commercial bubble wand that you have from a previous bottle of store-bought bubble solution, or you can use one side of a pair of old eyeglass frames with the lens removed, or you can form a loop out of a paper clip or wire hanger, or you can put the tips of your forefinger

Materials Needed

1/2 cup of dishwashing liquid, 3/4 gallon of water, two tablespoons of glycerine (ask for it at your drugstore counter), bowl, measuring cup, mixing spoon or other implement for stirring, and (these next items are all optional) eyeglass frames with a lens missing and/or paper clip and/or wire hanger and/or commercial bubble wand

and thumb together to form a circle (an "okay" sign), dip the entire circle into the bubble mixture, and softly blow into it or wave it gently through the air.

If there's any leftover bubble solution (unlikely, but possible), be sure to dispose of it (down the drain is fine) so that little kids or pets aren't tempted to drink it. Or if there's a substantial amount left, store it in a tightly closed jar, out of reach of small hands, as you would with any commercial bubble solution.

༈ 40 ༈
MOCK CALZONES

These calzones aren't authentic, but they're tasty and they're easy, and you and your daughter can make them together and then eat them together. Preheat your oven to 350°. Cut each roll in half, scoop out most of the inside, and fill the hollowed-out roll halves with the meat and cheese (and optional oregano and/or garlic powder). Wrap each roll half in aluminum foil securely (to prevent cheese drips) and place on the cookie sheet. Place the cookie sheet in the oven for about ten minutes. After ten minutes, remove the cookie sheet, open the aluminum foil enclosing one of the calzones, and make sure the cheese is melted. If it is, turn off the oven and serve the calzones. If not, rewrap the calzone and return the cookie sheet to the oven for another five or ten minutes.

When the calzones are ready, enjoy!

Materials Needed

One large bread roll for each of you, pepperoni and/or Italian salami (or sautéed vegetables), mozzarella and/or provolone, aluminum foil, cookie sheet, and (optional) oregano and/or garlic powder

TELLING TALES ... ABOUT YOUR DAUGHTER

Who doesn't like being "a star"? And that's especially true of kids, who, unless they're exceptionally shy, enjoy some form of limelight shining on them. Even if your daughter isn't an actress, doesn't put on puppet shows, doesn't enjoy singing, and knows nothing of ballet or other forms of dance, she can still "star" ... in a story, and it can help build self-confidence.

You can start out by telling the first story. Now, I am not talking about true "when-you-were-very-little" stories (those are good too — they're simply not what this activity is about), but rather fictional, made-up tales, in which your daughter is the heroine, but her life is very different from reality. Depending on what her interests are, or what type of tale you think will entertain her, you can make up a story about discovering that she's really the

Materials Needed

None

long-lost heir to the throne of Millania, and from now on she is to be known as Princess [her name goes here], and how she traveled to the kingdom of Millania and was met with a royal reception, and ... well, you make the rest of it up.

Or you can make up a story about your daughter and her favorite stuffed animal going into the woods and discovering a castle, in which a _____ was living. Or about your daughter finding a *huge* stack of money on the sidewalk, which nobody claims, so she gets to keep it, and she uses it to buy a house for all the cats and dogs who have nowhere to live, and moves into the house herself to take care of them. Or, speaking of animals, a story about her discovering a new species of animal that nobody ever knew about before. Or ....?

And then get *her* to make up a story about herself. Or several.

⸎ 42 ⸎

WHAT WOULD YOU DO WITH ...?

In the previous activity, I mentioned a story about your daughter finding a huge stack of money. This leads me to suggest still another activity the two of you can enjoy together: a thinking activity. Thinking activities are good ways to keep a restless child occupied on a car trip, in the doctor's waiting room, or in other "waiting" situations. They're also good to indulge in while you do chores together, as long as the chore is a mindless one and not one that requires concentration.

To start with, you can ask your daughter, "If you found a check for a million dollars on the sidewalk, what would you do with it?"

Other "What would you do with ...?" subjects include "a huge cardboard carton," "a vehicle that can drive on roads, sail on the water, and fly," "a pet llama" (for

Materials Needed

〰

Nothing but your daughter's imagination

kids old enough to know what a llama is) or "a pet giraffe," "your own private plane," "a machine that can instantly change the weather with the turn of a dial," or "a tower that reaches up to the sky."

Of course, there are plenty of other imagination-firing questions you can ask as well, such as, "If you could invent anything, what would you invent?" "If you could be anything in the world you wanted to be, what would you be?" or "If you could live in any kind of a house you wanted — any kind at all — tell me what it would be like."

≥ 43 ≤

TURNABOUT SALON

Washing your daughter's hair may be a chore, but playing salon? *Ahhh,* that's *fun.* And if your daughter gets to make *you* look "beautified," that can be even more fun. Well, that's the idea behind "Turnabout Salon": You each get to work on the other — both on the same day, or you can "beautify" your daughter one day, while she "beautifies" you

another time.

You can style each other's hair, paint and/or clip each other's nails, or toenails ... or all of these. Let her wash your hair and then style it to her liking. (Unless you have a particularly tricky hairstyle, you can always restore it before you are next seen in public.) I am not suggesting that you turn her loose with scissors, but for most women, your daughter can't do much harm with a comb and possibly a blow-dryer. And of course, you can style her hair as well.

But hair is not the only thing that gets worked on in a salon. You can give each other abbreviated manicures and pedicures as well. "Abbreviated"? Well, yes. I am not suggesting that either of you work on the other's cuticles, but you can certainly polish each other's nails — finger and/or toe — and you can clip your daughter's nails, even if she's still young enough

Materials Needed

Any of the following: Comb, shampoo and conditioner, blow-dryer, barrettes, nail polish (at least one color, and possibly several), nail clippers, cotton balls, nail polish remover

that she can't clip yours.

Try out an outrageous color of polish if you wish. Alternate coral nails with orange (fingers or toes, your nails or hers!), or paint them pink with a lilac stripe down the center. If you think the result is too bizarre to wear in public, have nail polish remover handy and explain that you were just playing, and that once the game is over, you need to restore her nails (or yours) to their former condition.

ৡ 44 ৢ
PLAY STORE

*Y*ou may already play store with your daughter, but you probably pretend to pick out some merchandise and then pretend to pay her, right? This time you're going to use real money ... and she's going to start to learn about the relative value of the different coins.

Since you're not playing with dollar

Materials Needed

Real coins in all denominations

bills or larger, this game will not teach her the real value of things. You may be buying a new shirt for 15¢ or a carton of milk for a quarter. But if you give her a quarter for that 15¢ shirt, will she understand that she owes you a dime in change? Does she know that five pennies equal a nickel? She'll start grasping the concept when she asks you for five cents for a pair of glasses and five cents for a new car, and you pay her one nickel for the one and five pennies for the other.

Don't expect her to learn all about money, the value of one coin relative to another, and how to make change all in one session of playing store. But if you continue to play with real money, the concepts will become more and more familiar to her.

⟩ 45 ⟨

PICTURE THIS STORY

To prepare for this pastime, cut out a number of magazine pictures. (These can include pictures cut from ads, if you want.) If you don't have many magazines lying around the house, use newspaper pictures, or even pictures from advertising flyers.

The pictures should all be of people, as diverse a collection as possible: men, women, boys, girls, executives, store clerks, people playing sports, people seated at the dinner table, people walking dogs .... You don't need one of each of the groups I've mentioned — they're just examples, to show you the diversity you want in the pictures you've cut out. Now put all the pictures in a large envelope.

Either you or your daughter removes one picture at random from the envelope (no peeking!). Now ask your daughter to make up a story about that person. If your daughter has trouble getting started with making up a story, ask her first to tell you a little about the person in the picture.

Suppose it's a man in shorts and a tennis shirt. You could ask your daughter what she thinks the man is doing: Is he on his way to work? Where might he work, dressed like that? Or is he more likely involved in some leisure activity? What might he be doing? (This activity sharpens your daughter's perception and ability to discern things about people by observing and drawing conclusions.) Once your daughter has come to a few conclusions about who the person is and what he or she might be doing, ask her again to tell you a story about the person.

Though there are no real rules for this activity, ideally the story should in some way relate to the picture, if there are any visual clues in the picture. A picture of a girl in a bathing suit should not inspire a story about a snowball fight. A picture of a woman with a dog doesn't have to inspire a story about the dog, but it shouldn't be about a woman riding a spaceship to the moon. A picture of a policeman might be about catching a burglar or preventing crime or finding a lost child, or it might even be about the policeman going home to his family; it shouldn't be about a professional football player.

At some point not too far along in the narrative, you'll take another picture out of the envelope and introduce another character into the story. Now your daughter has to interweave the second character into the story about the first. If the story seems to lag … or, conversely, if your daughter is going along just great and you think she's up for the challenge … introduce a third character to the story. And a fourth, if it seems appropriate. Your daughter is also free to dip into the envelope herself at any point that she decides a new character is needed.

She should continue spinning out the story till it has come to a logical end, or till she grows tired of it, or till there are so many plot twists and tangles that it's impossible to make headway and the plot has to be abandoned. While having fun, your daughter is sharpening her creativity and imagination.

) 46 (

PRINCESS FOR AN HOUR

If your daughter loves princess movies and books, she'll surely jump at the chance to be a princess for an hour. Unless you happen to be a real-life queen, or unless she grows up to marry a prince, your daughter isn't and

Materials Needed

At minimum, a paper (or other) crown, and a chair fixed up to look like a throne. Any other royal accoutrements will also add to the illusion ... and the fun.

won't ever be a princess ... but it's always fun to pretend!

So for just an hour, she can be Princess Stephanie/Brittany/Morgan/whatever her name is. You can be her advisor and helper, the Duchess, or Lady Thistlebottlethwait, or whatever role you want to assume. Ask her what sorts of proclamations she would like to put forth as princess. She can proclaim "Be Kind to Animals Week," or declare that everyone is to eat ice cream for lunch on the weekends ("a sundae every Sunday"), or order that all new house construction in the kingdom shall henceforth include an indoor swimming pool, or that all kitchen sinks dispense not only hot and cold water but also lemonade.

Of course, she can't really enforce some of these rules — you aren't going to let her Sunday lunch consist of nothing but ice cream ... but then, she isn't really a princess, either. Still, it's always fun to pretend!

﹩ 47 ﹟

FINGERPRINT DRAWINGS

The least-messy approach to fingerprint art is to use a standard inkpad with washable ink. If pads of various colors are available at your local office-supply store, great. (As an alternative, you can make a homemade ink pad by folding a paper towel several times over and soaking it with tempera paint.)

Practice fingerprinting first on a piece of scratch paper. You and your daughter will quickly learn that too much ink, or too much pressure, produces more of a mess than of a pattern, blurring the whorls and loops and lines that make up a fingerprint. When you've got the hang of it, it's time to proceed with your art project.

The most basic form of fingerprint drawing takes a single finger or thumb print and makes it the basis for some piece of drawn art. The print can become a head or a face, the body of a cat or dog, the fuselage of an airplane ... whatever suggests itself to each of you.

Materials Needed

Ink pad, paper, pencils or crayons or markers

You can put two or a whole handful of fingerprints

down on the paper and turn them into a person walking a dog, a classroom full of heads, a family of five. Three fingerprints stacked vertically can become a snowman; strung out horizontally, they might become a dachshund. Or four fingers could be a bunch of balloons held by a thumbprint that's turned into a person.

⸻ *48* ⸻
"I'M GOING SHOPPING"

Here's another game that requires no equipment, can be played anywhere, and is ideal for car trips, passing time while waiting in the supermarket checkout line, while doing chores together ... or just on its own as a fun game. It's for kids who are old enough to know the alphabet.

It doesn't matter which of you starts this memory game, but let's say it's you. You lead off by saying, "I'm going shopping and I'm buying _____" and finish the

Materials Needed

None

sentence with an item beginning with A: apples, perhaps, or even alligators ... it doesn't have to be an item you'd expect to find in the supermarket. Your daughter now continues with "I'm going shopping and I'm buying

_____"

and repeats your A item, adding a B item. She might say, "I'm buying apples and bananas." Now it's your turn again, and you'll repeat the A and B items and add a C item: "I'm going shopping, and I'm buying apples, bananas, and cars."

The first player who messes up, either by remembering the wrong item, or by saying one out of order, or by simply not remembering at all, is out of the game. The other player wins.

Don't worry about whether your daughter can think of X-rays or xylophones for X — it's highly doubtful that she or even you will be able to get that far, though you'll have a good time trying!

∂ 49 ¿

ALPHABET HOUSE

This is an activity for girls who know the alphabet, or it could be a great way to teach your daughter the alphabet. First write down all twenty-six letters of the alphabet, one below the other. (If you are using lined paper, each letter will appear on a separate line.) You can write the letters down yourself or have your daughter do it.

Now challenge your daughter to walk around the house looking for items that begin with each of the twenty-six letters, writing each word down as she spots the appropriate item. You'll accompany her and, if needed, prompt her a little. ("What does this start with?" or "What is this?" — touching the wall or the window when she despairs that nothing in the house begins with "W.") "Z" may be a tough letter to find if she doesn't own a toy zebra, but you may have a picture of one in a book somewhere, and a xylophone will provide the needed "X." "V" may be "vase," and "u" will likely be "umbrella." "Q" can

Materials Needed

Pen or pencil, notebook or paper

always be Q-Tip or the Queen in a deck of cards, and "Y" can be a yellow crayon.

More challenging variation for older daughters who are better spellers: Have your daughter look for objects that *end with* each letter of the alphabet.

❧ 50 ❧

PHOTO COLLAGE

*D*espite this being the age of digital photos, most of us still have plenty of old (or not-so-old) prints on hand. And ... let's face it ... some of these pictures are less than "picture perfect." But sometimes only part of the picture is disappointing. You can still cut out the good parts to use in this activity.

Then again, you may have only digital photos on hand, but if you have them stored on your computer, you can readily print out copies to use for a photo collage.

If your daughter is old enough to cut carefully around the people in the pictures, she can join you in cutting out the good images of family members; if not, she can still help with other parts of this project. Cut around those images you want to preserve: the head and body (or just the face) of anyone in the picture who came out right and whose image you want to use.

Materials Needed

☼

Scissors, paste, old photos that didn't come out quite right and/or printed copies of digital photos, construction paper, and/or cardboard (optional)

You can, if you choose, intersperse the cut-out faces or faces-and-bodies with construction paper cut-outs of hearts, letters of the alphabet (such as your family's last initial, or the first initial of each person pictured), or free-form shapes. You can also cut out a "frame" of brown construction paper. And perhaps your daughter can supply these construction-paper additions if she's not yet capable of cutting carefully around the images in the photos.

Now apply glue to the backs of the cut-outs — both photographic and construction paper — and artfully arrange them, either on a full sheet of construction paper or on a large sheet of cardboard, forming a collage with, if you wish, a construction-paper "frame" bordering the picture. Let your daughter help in deciding where each cut-out might go, and in carefully placing it on the collage.

♪ 51 ♪
JUNIOR ILLUSTRATOR

What child doesn't love to be read to? And often, kids want to be part of the read-aloud process … sometimes before they're old enough to read. But even if your daughter can't read yet, she can still participate … by supplying the pictures for a story.

First, pick out a story you can read to your daughter (or one you can tell her from memory). It can be a picture

book story, a story from a book without pictures, a story you remember well enough to retell, a story you've made up yourself, or even a family story that will hold her interest.

Now ask your daughter to illustrate it. *Hint:* If the story is one from a picture book, suggest that instead of drawing her own version of the pictures in the book, she draw pictures that illustrate other parts of the story that the book's original pictures don't cover.

❧ 52 ❧

DRAW YOUR FAMILY TREE

Family relationships can be hard to keep straight, especially in large families with many branches, or in today's spread-out families, where many family members are people your daughter has never met, or has met once at best. Just how is Cousin Carl related? If Aunt Martha is really a great-aunt but is called merely "Aunt," if there are both an Uncle Arthur and a Cousin Arthur (as there were in my family when I was a kid), if there are two Cousin Claires, if Aunt Elaine is younger than Cousin Stella, it can all get pretty confusing for even a twelve-year-old, let alone a six-year-old.

At minimum, I'm suggesting you draw a simple family tree for your daughter. Assuming you and your

Materials Needed

♕

Pen and paper, photos
of family members
(optional)

spouse don't come from large families, with lots of siblings and cousins, you can draw one family tree that shows both sides of the family, replete with the many relatives on each side, and dating back at least to Grandma and Grandpa on each side, if not further.

Draw separate trees for some of the branches, if necessary. (If Dad's sister's husband's brother and his wife, and their kids, are always part of family gatherings, you want to include them, but there may not be room on the main tree.)

If there's room, and you have the information, you can include year of birth, year of marriage, and year of death where appropriate; if you don't want to get that elaborate, the main thing is just to show who the family members are and how they're related. Once you've explained to your daughter how to "read" a family tree, seeing it on paper with all its connections will make the family relationships a lot easier to understand.

You may need to draw two — or more — separate family trees if there are many brothers and sisters, many cousins ... or several remarriages that have resulted in step- and half-relatives.

To give the tree even more impact, a small picture of each relative can be pasted above that person's name.

❧ 53 ❧
DRAW A FAMILY TIMELINE

For this one, you're going to need at least one l-o-o-o-n-g piece of paper. You can tape a number of 8-1/2" x 11" sheets of typing paper or construction paper end to end, or you can ask a local merchant with brown wrapping paper in long rolls (such as a butcher might have) for a long strip ... or two or three. (Why two or three? Because you might want to draw more than one timeline, and because you might make mistakes the first time and want to start over on a fresh piece of paper.)

There are several ways to approach this project:

⊙ You can draw a timeline with just your immediate family on it.

Materials Needed

A long piece of paper, pen

⊙ You can draw a timeline that goes back several generations.

⊙ You can include only family events on it.

⊙ You can include world and national news events too.

⊙ You can draw parallel timelines, one showing family events and the other showing events that took place in the larger world around us at the same time.

Let's start with the simplest timeline first — a timeline of your immediate family. You may want to use a two-colored system, though that's not necessary. Draw a straight horizontal line, marking off every five years in equal increments. Start the timeline over on the left-hand edge of the paper, with a vertical mark representing the beginning of the decade in which an event, say, your wedding, took place. So if you were married in 1984, your family's timeline would start with 1980, represented by a vertical mark. Label it.

Now mark off years in increments of five and label them. Leave plenty of room at the right for more years. And do all this in one color — say, black.

Now, in red, mark a vertical line in the appropriate place for each event in your family. A line inserted in red at the appropriate point for 1984 would be labeled (still in red) "1984. Mom & Dad married." Another line, at its appropriate juncture, would read, "1986. Jenny born." Another line, at 1988, would read, "1988. Max born." You might want a line reading "1992. Jenny starts elementary school." And so forth.

A more comprehensive — and compressed — timeline could go back several generations or even a century. It would show such events as "1880. Great-Great-Great-Grandma Mary arrives from Germany," "1901. Great-Great-Grandpa Lou born," "1958. Great-Great-Grandma Ross dies," "1959. Grandma and Grandpa O'Donnell get married," "1960. Dad born," among other notations. In cases like these, it's best to stick to immediate ancestors — parents, grandparents, great-grandparents, and farther back if desired, omitting great-aunts, cousins, and so forth.

On that same timeline, preferably in yet a different color, or else on a parallel timeline immediately below it, you can show major world events:

⊙ "World War I ends."

⊙ "Great Depression starts."

⊙ "World War II starts."

⊙ "JFK assassinated."

And so forth. The time markers and how many of

them you'll include is up to you.

Likewise, what other family events you'll include beyond immigrations, births, deaths, and marriages is entirely up to you. This will depend in part on the size of your family, how far back you're drawing your timeline, and how many events there have been. If any family member received a significant honor or had a major accomplishment, consider putting that on the timeline:

- ⊙ "Grandpa Larry's play produced."
- ⊙ "Dad gets his picture in national magazine."
- ⊙ "Family goes to Disney World."

This last entry can be deemed suitable for inclusion if the trip was a major event in the kids' lives, a once-in-a-lifetime trip.

A Family Timeline will help your daughter (and any other kids you have) get a better grasp on family history, and a better comprehension of how one event relates to another, time-wise. Including events of importance in the larger world, and showing them in relationship to family events, will help your daughter get a better grasp on recent history, too. And because she's going to help you draw the timeline, she'll remember even better the facts and dates shown on it.

♪ 54 ♪

STARE-DOWN

All that's required in this silly, simple pastime is for you and your daughter to stare into each other's eyes and try not to blink … or to giggle, grin, talk, or move. Whoever does any of those things first is out of the game, and the other is the winner. Silly? Yes. Simple? Also yes. And fun for your daughter? Definitely yes!

Materials Needed

None

A variation on this is "Don't Laugh," in which each

of you tries to make the other laugh — one at a time — by making goofy faces or perhaps telling jokes. The first one to make the other laugh is the winner.

♪ 55 ♪

BECAUSE IT'S HER CAUSE

We already talked about walking for a cause ("Locomotion Commotion," page 44), but there are other ways for you and your daughter to work together to help a cause that's important to her.

Many kids today, once they're old enough to understand the works of charitable and/or socially active organizations, become caught up in one or more such organizations' cause. The most popular seem to be environmental organizations and animal-rights organizations, but kids with a close relative who has or has had a particular medical condition are sometimes drawn to the organization that fights that specific disease or condition.

If your daughter has begun admiring the work of Greenpeace, a local food bank, or any other organization, or if she is impassioned about the cause that such a

Materials Needed

Depending on the course of action you choose, computer and printer and paper, and/or phone, and/or crafts materials

group espouses, suggest that she — with your help — do something meaningful in support of that organization's work.

What that "something meaningful" will be depends on the group, what their current needs are, and where her talents and abilities lie. Here are some possibilities:

⊙ Collect money (from neighbors and/or in school from her friends) for the organization.

⊙ Organize a letter-writing campaign in support of a group's current effort.

⊙ Circulate a petition.

⊙ Do volunteer work at the organization's office if they are a local cause or a national cause with a local office.

Having you volunteer to work alongside your daughter on a cause that she cares about will be meaningful to her.

ʃ 56 ʃ
SMOOTH(IE) MOVES

Smoothies are popular, easy to make, tasty, and a good way to get kids to eat fruit. They are also fun to make ... and to create (that is, to dream up an original recipe for). There are fruit smoothies (the most popular), veggie smoothies, even chocolate smoothies ... and more.

Why simply follow someone else's recipe when it's so much more fun to dream up your own?

Decide whether you're going to whip up a fruit smoothie, veggie smoothie, or other type (e.g., honey, chocolate, brown sugar). Select the ingredients you want to use, and decide how much you think you want to use of each one. Write down your ingredients and the trial quantity of each. Place the desired amount of each ingredient in the blender ... and press the button. When the smoothie is ... smooth, pour out a little and taste it.

If it's delicious as-is, great! Drink up, while you decide on a name for

Materials Needed

Blender and assorted smoothie ingredients (to be determined by the two of you)

your very own concoction.

On the other hand, if, as is very likely, you think you need a tad more mango, some OJ for tartness, or a couple of teaspoons of honey for sweetness, add what you think is needed, write it down on the paper on which you wrote the original recipe, give the blender another whirl ... and it's time to taste your concoction again.

Not every recipe will be a winner. That's why the method is called "trial and error." There are always errors. But there are also always winners. Discard the recipes that don't come out right no matter what you add, and keep the ones that prove ultimately delicious and satisfying. It's your own creation! The two of you devised it, named it ... and can be proud of it.

❦ 57 ❦

HOOP-DE-DOO

*Y*ou can make your own hula hoops out of irrigation tubing and duct tape. Cut the tubing to a suitable length and attach the two ends together with the duct tape. Use just enough tape to do the job; you don't want to overweight the joint and thus make your hoops off balance.

Once you've created two hoops, one for each of you, you can learn (or practice remembering) how to keep a hula hoop circling around your waist without it falling to the ground. When you've both got the hang of it, have a contest and see which of you can keep her hula hoop going longer.

Materials Needed

Irrigation tubing, duct tape

THE ⎯⎯⎯⎯⎯⎯⎯⎯⎯⎯⎯ FAMILY BOOK CLUB

There are many ways to organize a family book club. Your daughter's age will be one of the factors helping you decide how to do it. The book club can simply consist of you and your daughter taking regular trips to the library and each selecting books that appeal to you. (Naturally, these days libraries offer many other materials than just books, but while she may choose to borrow CDs, DVDs, or other materials while she is there, the primary purpose behind this activity — besides togetherness — is reading.)

Ramp it up a notch and hold "book club meetings" at home at which you each discuss the relative merits of the books you've each borrowed, before returning them to the library and borrowing others.

You can even each write a review of each book you borrow, or your favorite book of the week, and read these reviews to each other.

Materials Needed

Library card and (optional) paper and pen or computer

"Favorite Things" Poster

Materials Needed

Poster board, picture of you, picture of your daughter, three different colored marking pens plus black marking pen, glue

You and your daughter often don't agree ... right? Like all mothers and daughters, you have certainly got your differences ... over what foods you prefer, what music you like best, how you like to dress, and ... well, just about everything. But as she matures (and you too!), you can learn to respect each other's differences. And you can also find common ground on which you agree.

So, here's the deal: You're going to make a poster on which you'll show your individual favorite things ... and the ones on which you agree, as well.

At the top of a large piece of poster board, write Our Favorite Things in black. Down the left side of the poster board, also in black, write such categories as Music, Song, Food, Dance, Singer, Author, Place to Go, Restaurant, and whatever other categories you wish to add. To the right of that, glue a picture of yourself (just the face is fine) and label it MOM in one color — let's say red. To the right of that, glue a picture of your daughter and label it with her name in a different color — let's say blue.

Now fill in the categories for each of you. Mom, fill in your favorites in your color, while your daughter fills in her favorites in her color. But when you happen to agree, use the third color — let's say purple, which is, of course, a blend of red and blue.

⟩ 60 ⟨

MEALS FROM THE HEART

It's never too early for your daughter to learn about the importance of helping others. This activity can be very pleasurable and heartwarming, and you and your daughter will have fun working side by side.

Choose a beneficiary of your efforts: a relative, friend, or neighbor who has limited mobility. This may be someone older, someone in ill health, or someone who for whatever reason cannot easily (if at all) spend much time in his or her kitchen or get out to a restaurant

Materials Needed

✿

Whatever you need to cook a simple meal, plus suitable containers to carry the meal in.

Optional: A bright ribbon bow (which can be pre-tied or one you tie yourself)

or to the store for a prepared meal. Bearing in mind this person's physical issues (does he have poor teeth and need only soft foods; does she have health conditions that require her to avoid salt or sugar?), plan anything from one dish to a whole dinner (main course, veggie, starch, and possibly dessert) that seems suitable. Keep in mind that the recipient of your kindness may actually prefer simpler foods. It is not necessary to cook anything elaborate. A simple, healthy, hearty meal (or single dish) will be very welcome. It could be something as basic as a container of chicken salad or a small pork roast or a meat loaf or broiled chicken. Avoid choosing something that has to be served piping hot unless the recipient lives in very close proximity. And do choose something that your daughter can get

✿

111

actively involved in the preparation of.

If you wish, you can take your daughter shopping with you when you go to buy the necessary ingredients. Or her involvement can begin when you actually start preparing the food. As you work together in the kitchen, talk about how your neighbor, friend, or relative is going to enjoy getting a good home-cooked meal (or single dish), and how good it is for people to help each other.

When the dish or meal is all ready, packaged in containers (or aluminum foil, or whatever's appropriate), placed in a shopping bag, in a basket, or on a tray, and ready to transport, you can add a pretty colored ribbon bow to the handles of the shopping bag or basket, or place a single flower on the tray if you want, and then the two of you can take the food to its intended recipient.

Alternative: Rather than delivering a meal or main dish, you can bake cookies, a cake, or muffins together and deliver that.

♪ 61 ♪
"WHEN I WAS A LITTLE GIRL"

*E*very child loves bedtime stories. But these are *special* bedtime stories. These aren't just stories of the Big Bad Wolf, or trolls, or elves, or even princesses. These are stories of *you* ... when you were younger. These bedtime stories are "Me Stories" ... stories of when you were a child.

Young children are amazed to hear their moms were ever little. In their minds, mommies were always mommies. Somewhat older girls know their moms were once kids ... though it often blows them away to consider that possibility. Amuse your daughter by telling her stories of when you were a little girl. What amused you then? What upset you? What concerned you? What was fun for you? What did your parents do to keep you busy and happy? What were your favorite games? What chores did you hate the most?

Materials Needed

None

BEACH-IN-A-JAR

This activity requires proximity to a beach, whether you live near the shore or are just visiting. Take your daughter beach walking, and bring an empty canning jar with you. Put a layer of sand into the jar and wedge small rocks or driftwood into the sand. Then add shells, and finally fill the jar with seawater. Screw the lid on tightly, and transport it home carefully.

When you get home, fill a saucepan with water and place the jar in the saucepan. Leave the jar in simmering water for fifteen minutes. This will eliminate any algae in the jar. Remove the jar from the water (do this yourself, Mom) and allow it to cool before your daughter places it proudly on display in her room (or in the family room or living room).

Materials Needed

Canning jar, sand, rocks and/or small driftwood, shells, seawater, saucepan

} 63 {

COMPARISON REVIEWERS

The idea here is to find a book that's been made into a movie (*Charlie and the Chocolate Factory,* for example, for a younger daughter, or *Dr. Dolittle,* or one of the Harry Potter books), and have both of you read the book, then both watch the movie together (most probably on DVD, though possibly in a movie theatre), and then discuss and compare the two.

Materials Needed

Book and movie derived therefrom that are suitable for your daughter's age

Here are some suggested topics for discussion: Was the movie true to the book? Better or not as good? Did the actors stay true to the characters? Was the ending the same, and if not, was it better or not as satisfying? How do you feel about any parts of the book that may have been omitted in the movie — scenes or subplots, for example? Was anything added to the movie that wasn't in the book, and how do you each feel about that? Do you think you would feel differently if you had seen the movie before reading the book instead of vice versa?

TREAT YOURSELVES TO A "DATE" (WITH PEANUT BUTTER)

Whether you eat these as dessert or a snack, they're a sweet treat and easy to make, and you and your daughter can have fun preparing them together.

By purchasing pitted dates, you eliminate the tedious step of removing the pits from the dates.

If the pitting machine has not made a large enough incision in the dates, you, Mom, will need to slit the dates with a knife sufficiently so that your daughter can insert approximately one teaspoon (amount need not be precise) of peanut butter into each date.

On a clean countertop, a rolling board, or a piece of either waxed paper or aluminum foil, sprinkle some sugar (don't overdo it) and roll each peanut-butter-

Materials Needed

Pitted dates, peanut butter (approx. 1 teaspoon per date used — creamy or chunky style, cook's choice), knife, sugar, wax paper

stuffed date in the sugar. On a fresh piece of waxed paper or aluminum foil, stack the dates after you have sugar-coated them, and when you have prepared all the dates you'd like, place the stacked pile in the freezer. (Not only do they taste much better frozen, but freezing them also reduces the choking hazard associated with eating peanut butter that hasn't been moistened with jelly.)

Obviously this is not an activity to be engaged in by those with peanut or nut allergies.

65
SHALL WE DANCE?

Which dance moves were popular when you were younger? Your daughter might think "your" dances are funny ... but she also might enjoy learning them. And since kids love "teaching Mommy," she'll probably be happy to teach you the dances she and her friends enjoy ... and/or her

Materials Needed

Music source (such as an MP3 player, CD player, radio, or music video station)

own special moves and dance steps that she has developed and perfected.

So put on the music and show each other your best moves.

⸎ 66 ⸎

LEARN THE ART OF NAPKIN FOLDING

Virtually everyone knows the two basic methods of napkin folding: You can fold the napkin in half along an imaginary center line to create a rectangle, or you can fold it so that two diagonally opposite corners meet, creating a triangle. But there are so many fancy and intricate folds also possible — some designed to have the napkin sitting beside or on top of the dinner plate, others intended to make the napkin "blossom" like a flower and rest either in an empty stemware glass or alongside the plate. Then there is a method of folding that creates a pocket in which the utensils are inserted.

If you and/or your daughter are easily frustrated by trying to figure out these folds on your own, there are instructions available on the Web and in books that your library may have. But if you don't have a low frustration tolerance, it's more fun to figure out intricate and interesting folds on your own. Without competing to see who comes up with the best fold, the most attractive folds, or the first good fold, you and your daughter can work alongside each other, each trying to come up with a good result from fancy folding. When one of you devises a good decorative fold, teach it to the other ... and continue trying to find some more good folds.

≥ 67 ≤
"LET'S PAINT YOUR ROOM"

Materials Needed

Paint, two rollers with long handle extensions, one small brush (for cutting in corners and working on window frames and closet door frames), two roller pans, drop cloths (or you can sub old newspapers), stepladder

What child doesn't want her room painted? Your daughter might want to try out a new color on her walls, and if you're up for it, you can help her do the painting

herself. You can both work simultaneously with rollers, adding handle extensions to reach up to the ceiling. You work on one wall while she works on another. Give yourself the task of climbing the ladder to cut in with a brush up next to the ceiling.

Your daughter will enjoy her newly painted room and will have the additional pleasure of being able to say, "I did it myself." (With a little help from Mom.)

⸎ 68 ⸎
WHAT MAKES IT TICK?

Gadgets and gizmos and gears, oh my. Did you just buy a new phone or clock? What are you going to do with the old one? How about you and your daughter take it apart to see how it works? But you don't have to wait till you buy new electronic or mechanical items and thereby obsolesce the old ones. You can buy used gadgets at the flea market or a yard sale to "perform surgery on."

Hint: The more mechanical and less electronic the gadget is, the more apparent its mechanisms will be. There's not much to see in a device made up largely of circuit boards. You'll do better with one that relies on gears or cogs or flywheels or all of

Materials Needed

Any mechanical objects that you can afford to part with or that you pick up at a yard sale or flea market for the express purpose of taking them apart, screwdrivers and perhaps other tools for disassembling the gadgets you're going to be investigating these … like a wind-up travel clock, a kitchen timer, or a wind-up toy.

Not that there's anything wrong with appliances and other gadgets that are mainly electronic. They can be fun to investigate too. But their method of working will be less transparent.

Warning: some electronic components may contain toxins, so don't smash open small parts, and be sure to wash up carefully afterward.

Bonus activity for older girls: Save the taken-apart parts from several different gadgets and see if the two of you can assemble some of these into a new contraption. Even if your newly created doohickey doesn't serve any serious purpose, if you can get it to tick, or inch forward, or spray water, or perform any other function, you'll have the fun and satisfaction of any beginning inventor.

♪ 69 ♪
Magic Garden
of Jupiter

Unless your daughter is reasonably older — perhaps ten or so — it will be better if you do most or all of the set-up yourself for this activity while she watches. Then let her enjoy the results. Here's what you do:

Pour the liquid bluing into the bowl. Add enough salt that the mixture is a thick, grainy liquid. Add a drop or two of food coloring, if you wish. Put the charcoal briquet or piece of coal in the middle of the aluminum pie plate. Slowly drizzle the salt-and-bluing mixture onto it, trying to keep most of it on top of the briquet rather than letting it run into the pie pan. Add a little water in the bottom of the pan. Be sure to pour the water

Materials Needed

Two tablespoons liquid bluing (available in the section of the supermarket where you find laundry soap and bleach), salt, one piece of coal or charcoal briquet, water, food coloring (optional), disposable aluminum pie pan, bowl, spoon, measuring spoons.

around the briquet rather than onto it. You don't want to wash the salt-and-bluing mixture off the briquet. Place the pie plate in a place where you can safely leave it for a while.

This place should not be:

⊙ One where a pet or young child could reach it and ingest any of the ingredients.

⊙ On fine furniture or any other surface that might be harmed by spillage. The growth pattern of a Magic Garden of Jupiter is unpredictable. It *could* grow over the edge of the pie plate and some *might* fall to the surface below.

⊙ Somewhere where it might be bumped and jarred by someone. A Magic Garden of Jupiter is fragile and breaks easily.

Keep an eye on your creation. Within an hour, your Magic Garden will begin to grow. It will sprout spires, odd growths, and fascinating shapes. No two Magic Gardens grow alike. (In fact, it's interesting to create *two* Magic Gardens of Jupiter side by side and observe the differences between the two. Although you've created them in exactly the same way, they won't come out identically.)

❧ 70 ❧

A CLOSE-KNIT FAMILY

Seems as if everyone's knitting these days ... including many celebrities. Everything old is new again, and Great-Great-Grandma's favorite pastime is enjoying a new vogue. So join in the fun ... and become "knit-wits."

If you already know how to knit, you're two steps ahead of the game and only have to teach your daughter. If you're not already a knitter, you can learn right along with her. Many crafts shops, yarn shops, or sewing shops offer knitting lessons (often free), which you and your daughter can attend together before wielding the needles. If there are no lessons offered in your area, or if you just prefer learning at your own speed, borrow a library book that teaches knitting, or download instructions from the Web.

Once you master the basics, you can learn the intricacies and fancy work. And, whatever level each of you

Materials Needed
✻

Knitting needles, wool, and possibly instructions (if you are not already knitting-knowledgeable)

is at, you can have regular or irregular "knitting circles" for two, when you sit, knit, chat, and compare your handiwork.

❧ 71 ❧

LIVING ROOM CAMP-OUT

Some living arrangements don't allow for camping out in the backyard. But you can still camp out in the living room.

Whether or not you'll put up a tent (if you own one) depends on how much furniture you want to move and how realistic you want the experience to be. In any event, you can sleep in bedrolls, on air mattresses, in sleeping bags, or simply on sheets spread out on the floor.

There will be no TV tonight. Your entertainment will consist of telling ghost stories around a flashlight "campfire," reading comic books by flashlight, exchanging stories in the encouraging secrecy of utter darkness, and perhaps nibbling trail mix or some other suitable camp-out food. (You'll have to forgo the s'mores or roasted marshmallows — a campfire in the living room is hardly an option!)

Make sure that not only are all the living room lights turned off but so are the lights in any adjacent room or hallway. Re-create the darkness of a woods or field by night, to simulate the camp-out experience as closely as possible. There is no moon out tonight, not even stars to light your way, but each of you has a flashlight in case of a need to get up in the middle of the night.

Materials Needed

Bedrolls or air mattresses or sleeping bags or sheets and pillows, flashlights, trail mix or other suitable camp-out food, and comic books.
Optional: Tent

ᔥ 72 ᔥ

WORDMATCH

This game requires that your daughter be old enough to spell simple words. It's a game for two to four players, so once you've played it with your daughter, and she's learned how, she can play it with her friends, or you can include the rest of the family, on a later occasion.

Before you play for the first time, your daughter can have fun helping you prepare the needed materials for the game. There are six picture cards. All should be the same size, a size large enough for your daughter to draw a picture on and to spell the word underneath. The six picture cards are HOUSE, PEACH, CLOWN, MUSIC, SMILE, and QUILT.

There are 30 letter cards, distribution of which is as follows:

A: 1; C: 3; E: 3; H: 2; I: 3; L: 3; M: 2; N: 1; O: 2; P: 1; Q: 1; S: 3; T: 1; U: 3; W: 1. They need to be just large enough for your daughter to handle them comfortably. All the letter cards need to be uniform in size, so there is no telling which is which from the back. This

Materials Needed

Enough cardboard to create six picture cards and thirty letter cards, scissors, crayons or markers, and two books or something similar against which each player can lean her letter cards, in lieu of a letter-card holder (like the tile racks in Scrabble)

probably means that you ought to do the cutting, even though your daughter can write the letters.

Now to actually play:

Shuffle all the picture cards and place them face-down, either in a pile or spread out. Each player picks one picture card, placing it face-up in front of herself. Put the unused picture cards away.

Shuffle all the letter cards by placing them face-down on the table and moving them around. Leave them spread out, face-down, on the table. Each player picks six letter cards and places them against a book or similar holder that will keep them upright so the player can see them without her opponent seeing them.

Choose one player to start. (You can choose by rock-paper-scissors, a roll of dice, or any other method you prefer.) Play alternates between players thereafter. (In a game with more than two players, play moves around the table clockwise.)

The first player picks a letter card. She has the

option of taking one from the center of the table or taking one from her opponent. (In a three-or-more-player game, she is free to pick from any opponent.) After looking at her new acquisition, she must then discard any one letter card onto the center of the table and shuffle by moving the tiles around.

If she took the letter card from among your cards, you now take a card from the center (not from her hand).

Play continues in turn, with each player taking one letter from either the table or her opponent, and then discarding a letter and shuffling. Each turn consists of taking only one letter, whether or not the player gets a letter she needs.

Replenishing your stock after an opponent has removed one card from your hand does not count as a turn.

The object of the game is to get all five tiles you need to spell the word on your picture card. It is not advisable to make delighted faces, or otherwise let your opponent know that you are closer to your goal. She may then decide to play defensively and take cards from your hand. You cannot protect the cards in your hand. If your opponent chooses to pick one you need, she may do so.

When you have all the letters you need to spell your word, yell out "Wordmatch!" and place your letters right-side-up next to your picture card, to show that you are correct. The first one to do so wins the game.

Variation: Players in a two-handed game may agree in advance to play two word cards at once. They still get only six letter cards each. When a player matches all five letters on one of her picture cards, she yells out "Wordmatch!" and places that picture face-up along with the five appropriate letter tiles face-up too. Those tiles cannot now be taken by her opponent. However, the game progresses from there, with the player who just put down the cards now picking up five more letter cards, as the winner is the first player to spell out *both* pictures she has picked.

❧ 73 ❦
CAR-WASH CAPERS

Car-washing: To you it's a chore to be accomplished as seldom as possible and as quickly as possible. But to your daughter? It's a "grown-up" activity (which automatically makes it fun), *and* it's a sanctioned opportunity to get as wet as can be

Materials Needed

Soap, water hose, rags

without parental repercussions. (Watch out. You're likely to get wet too!)

On a very warm day, dress in your bathing suits for this activity. Otherwise, just wear clothes that won't be any the worse for getting wet and/or soapy. Turn the activity into even more fun by letting your daughter spell out her name in soapsuds, or otherwise create soapy "art" before you get down to the serious business of wetting the car down, washing it thoroughly, and rinsing it off.

§ 74 §

JOINT ACTS OF KINDNESS

Practice Random Acts of Kindness: Has that ever been your mantra, or at least a slogan you wanted to act on more often? How does your daughter feel about it? Start this activity with a discussion about how good it feels to be a day-brightener for someone else, and how doing so doesn't have to involve anything elaborate, time-consuming, or expensive.

We've already talked about delivering meals to an older or disabled relative or neighbor (Meals from the Heart, page 110), and that's certainly an act of kindness, but there are other things you can do for people that will help them feel better about their day.

How about smiling at a stranger in

Materials Needed

Usually none, occasionally varied materials according to the good deed you choose

the store you're shopping in — perhaps the woman in line in front of you at the checkout — and offering some pleasantry about the weather or some other neutral subject? Or helping someone cross the street who looks like she could use some assistance? Or  taking your old, already-read, ready-to-be recycled magazines to a shut-in neighbor, or the local Veterans Affairs facility, or senior citizens' activities center? What about delivering some canned goods to a local food bank?

You can choose one day a week to perform a Random Act of Kindness, or you can simply pledge to do at least one such act a week. Then report to each other, each week, on what you did, if you didn't do it together. If you did perform your Random Act of Kindness together, you can still discuss what you did, how you think the recipient felt, and what next week's RAK might be.

₰ 75 ₰
WHAT'S THE GOOD WORD?

This could qualify as a Random Act of Kindness (see previous activity), but it's such an important activity that it really deserves an entry of its own. My grandmother always advocated telling people what you like about them, complimenting people on their good points, speaking up, and letting them hear deservedly nice things about themselves. Naturally, this can be done literally that way — spoken aloud, as my grandmother advocated — but I'm a believer in putting nice things in writing. A short note is a "keeper," something you can file away to re-read whenever your day could use a lift.

Materials Needed

Paper and either pen or computer

So what I'm suggesting here is that you and your daughter talk about the nice people you know, and that you then sit down together to write a note from both of you, or one note from each of you, to a person (or two different people, with each of you writing to someone different), thanking that person for being extra-kind or pleasant, or for a specific kind act or gesture on that person's part. The note doesn't have to be at all long or formal. All you really need to say is, "Dear _____, I wanted to write this note to tell you how much I/we appreciate _____." And then list this particular nice trait of hers, or the specific thing she did once or does regularly that you think is worthy of recognition.

The note will not only serve as a day-brightener for the recipient but also as a reminder to your daughter of how meaningful it can be to others when you take the time to be extra-nice to people.

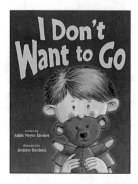

Don't Squash That Bug!
The Curious Kid's Guide to Insects
by Natalie Rompella
ISBN: 978-1-897073-50-6

Once kids discover how amazing insects can be, they'll go from squashing bugs to studying them up close.

"...before your little bookworm can say 'Ewww', arm her with a little bit of knowledge and she might be less likely to squeal at the first ant sighting ... a swarm of intriguing facts about all types of insects ..." – *The Chronicle Herald*

Oliver Has Something to Say!
by Pamela Edwards,
illustrated by Louis Pilon
ISBN: 978-1-897073-52-0

Each time Oliver opens his mouth to speak, his chatty parents and bossy sister answer for him. What does Oliver really want to say?

"... your child will beg you to read it again and again." – *The Literary Word*

"... shows shy kids the benefits of speaking up." – *Montreal Families*

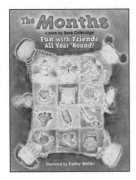

The Months:
Fun with Friends All Year 'Round!
a poem by Sara Coleridge,
illustrated by Kathy Weller
ISBN: 978-1-897073-67-4

Learn the months of the year through rhyming verse – part of the "Read Me a Poem" series.

"... a classic among poetry for the younger set ... made new with vivid and imaginative illustrations [that] depict children enjoying the joys of nature ..." – *CM: Canadian Review of Materials*

Also available from Lobster Press:

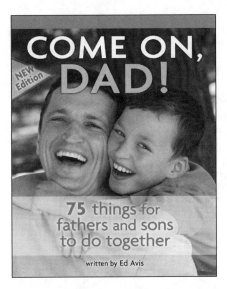

Come on, Dad!
75 Things for Fathers and Sons to Do Together
by Ed Avis
New Edition
ISBN: 978-1-897073-77-3

Dads are famous for being fun, but even the most creative father can use some new ideas for activities! This collection of 75 games, projects, recipes, and experiments will make memories that last long after the book is closed. Activities suited for boys ages 4 - 8 (and their dads).

"... offers everyday ways to nurture the parent-child bond."
– Publishers Weekly

"... helps turn Father-and-Son's Day into every day of the year."
– Georgia Parent